TO LOOSE
ALL PLUMS

TO LOOSE
ALL PLUMS

CAROLINE MACLEOD

To order additional copies of this book, contact:
Xlibris
800-056-3182
www.Xlibrispublishing.co.uk
Orders@Xlibrispublishing.co.uk
736746

CONTENTS

THE LOOSE ALL PLUMS ix
FOREWORD xi

VODKA RUM PUNCH..1
RUM PUNCH..1
COFFEE LIQUEUR PUNCH 2
HAM..3
VEGETABLE SOUP 4
CHRISTMAS DINNER 5
VEGETARIAN CHRISTMAS 7
CHRISTMAS PUDDING..9
BRANDY WHITE SAUCE 10
BRANDY BUTTER OR RUM BUTTER......................................11
LAST MINUTE CHRISTMAS CAKE 12
MINCE PIES...13
RUM TRIFLE 14
TOFFEED ORANGES..15
CHOCOLATE FUDGE CAKE 16
SULTANA AND VANILLA CHEESECAKE 17
CHOCOLATE FUDGE CHEESECAKE......................................18
CHOCOLATE FUDGE COOKIES..19

THE LOOSE ALL PLUMS SECTION 2

FRIED STEAK WITH MUSHROOM SAUCE............................23

TURKEY FRICASSE..24

TAGLIATELLE WITH WHITE FISH 25

BOILED EGGS...26

SMOKED HADDOCK CURRY..27

SAUSAGE AND TOMATO CURRY 28

EGG CURRY 29

CURRIED TOMATO AND AUBERGINE................................... 30

CURRIED POACHED SALMON..31

MAYONNAISE..32

FISHCAKES 33

SPAGHETTI WITH HAM AND CHEESE................................... 35

RICE WITH MUSHROOMS AND CREAM SAUCE 36

SCRAMBLED EGGS..37

POTATO SOUP 38

CARROT AND GINGER SOUP 39

CHICKEN LIVER PATE 40

MONKFISH CURRY 41

THE LOOSE ALL PLUMS SECTION 3

WALNUT AND HAZELNUT GALETTE....................................... 45

STRAWBERRY MERINGUE 46

PEACHES AND CUSTARD CREAM...47

BLACK CHERRY AND CHOCOLATE SPONGE 48

MELTED TOFFEE AND A WHIRL OF STRAWBERRY 49

BLACKCURRANT AND BANANA ROSE DESSERT 50

DATE AND GINGER CAKE...51

CARROT AND PINEAPPLE CAKE...52

WALNUT AND HAZELNUT ORANGE CAKE............................ 53

DROP SCONES 54

ALMOND COFFEE CAKE.. 55

CHOCOLATE ROULADE...56

FREEZER ICECREAM 57

A RULER'S BIRTHDAY CAKE.. 58

THE LOOSE ALL PLUMS SECTION 4

SHEPHERDS PIE...61

SPAGHETTI WITH MEAT SAUCE...62

CAULIFLOWER CHEESE.. 63

MACARONI CHEESE... 64

STEAK AND KIDNEY PIE 65

CHICKEN AND MUSHROOM PIE 66

FISH PIE...67

SALMON WITH PASTA 68

MACARONI WITH WHITE WINE AND HERB SAUCE 69

TUNA AND PIMENTO AND BEAN SALAD..70

PHEASANT STEW 71

PHEASANT AND BANANA CREAM 72

THE LOOSE ALL PLUMS

FOR YOUR MEASUREMENTS PLEASE USE A LITTLE GUESSWORK.

I AM A GREEDY COOK AS A FLAVOUR.

I HAVE WORKED FOR FAMILIES FOR SEVERAL YEARS AS A HOUSEKEEPER/COOK AND HAVE ALSO WORKED IN TWO HOTELS. I WOULD LIKE TO TEACH WHAT I KNOW ABOUT COOKING BECAUSE I THINK IT IS OF AN INVALUABLE INSIGHT WHICH LETS YOU KNOW HOW I KNOW WHAT I KNOW.

I AM GENEROUS AND HONEST AND KNOW A FEW MORE PENNIES SPENT ON YOUR DINNERS ONCE OR TWICE A WEEK WILL MAKE ALL THE DIFFERENCE TO YOUR NATURAL HEALTH.

FOREWORD

THERE IS A SENSE OF HOW TO COOK AND JUST USING THE SIMPLEST IDEAS AND FOOD THAT WORKS TOGETHER.

THIS COOKING BOOK GIVES YOU AN INSIGHT IN TO COOKING AND TELLS YOU FROM THE BASICS ONWARDS WHAT I KNOW.

I STARTED TO LEARN ABOUT COOKING AT HOME AND THEN WENT ON TO A COOKERY SCHOOL BY NOTTINGHAM WHICH TOLD ME "FURTHER ON THAN THAT THEN" AND THEY SAID THEN "TRY TO BE AT YOUR BEST THEN".

VODKA RUM PUNCH

LEMONADE 4 LITRES

VODKA 1 ½ LITRES

RUM 1 LITRE

SCHNAPPS ½ LITRE

STRAWBERRIES AND SATSUMAS

COCONUT MILK 3 CANS

RUM PUNCH

RUM 1 ½ LITRES

GIN ½ LITRE

ORANGE JUICE 3 LITRES

WHISKY 1 LITRE

TONIC WATER 1 ½ LITRES

4 LEMONS

CAROLINE MACLEOD

COFFEE LIQUEUR PUNCH

PERCOLATED COFFEE 3 LITRES

GIN 1 LITRE

RUM 2 LITRES

BRANDY ½ LITRE

SINGLE CREAM 60 FLUID OUNCES

FULL CREAM MILK 40 FLUID OUNCES

HAM

CLOVES
1 GAMMON JOINT
BAYLEAF
PEPPERCORNS
DIJON MUSTARD
DEMARARA SUGAR

PLACE THE HAM IN A BOWL OF WATER OVERNIGHT TO SOAK IN THE REFRIDGERATER.

THE NEXT DAY PLACE THE PEPPERCORNS IN WATER AND ADD HAM. BRING TO A GENTLE SIMMER AND CONTINUE TO SIMMER FOR 1 ½ HOURS. THE WATER HAS TO COVER THE HAM. COOL IN THE WATER.

REMOVE FROM THE PAN. SLICE OFF SKIN LEAVING ALL OF THE WHITE FAT UNDERNEATH THE SKIN, ON THE HAM.

CRISSCROSS THE MEAT IN A DIAMOND PATTERN WITH A KNIFE. PUT A CLOVE IN EACH DIAMOND SQUARE AND SPREAD OVER WITH THE DIJON MUSTARD AND SUGAR MIXTURE.

BAKE IN OVEN AT 220 CENTIGRADE UNTIL A CRUST IS FORMED. THIS SHOULD TAKE NO LONGER THAN 10 – 12 MINUTES.

VEGETABLE SOUP

BAYLEAF

2 CARROTS PEELED AND ROUGHLY CHOPPED

2 RED ONIONS PEELED AND ROUGHLY CHOPPED

2 CELERY STICKS ROUGHLY CHOPPED INCLUDING THE LEAVES

2 MEDIUM POTATOES PEELED AND ROUGHLY CHOPPED

2 COURGETTES SLICED ROUGHLY

SALT AND PEPPER

CHICKEN STOCK 3 PINTS

ADD VEGETABLES TO OIL IN PAN AND SAUTE AND AFTER 10 MINUTES ADD STOCK AND BOIL UNTIL VEGETABLES ARE WELL COOKED.

PUREE AND DILUTE WITH BOILING WATER TO DESIRED CONSISTENCY.

CHRISTMAS DINNER

TURKEY 18 – 20 LBS WITH STUFFING – 6 HOURS COOKING TIME AT 220 CENTIGRADE

TURKEY 12 – 14 LBS WITH STUFFING – 4 ½ HOURS IN THE OVEN AT 220 CENTIGRADE

COVER THE TURKEY WITH BACON AND COVER WITH SILVER FOIL

PUT ALL THE ROOT VEGETABLES ON TOP OF EACH OTHER MIXED UP IN A ROASTING PAN, COVER WITH VEGETABLE OIL AND SALT AND PEPPER AND ROAST FOR 2 HOURS ABOVE THE TURKEY IN THE OVEN.

YOU CAN ADD YOUR SAUSAGES WRAPPED WITH BACON ON TOP OF THE VEGETABLES 1 ½ HOURS BEFORE THE END OF THE COOKING TIME.

BUY THESE THINGS TO EASE COOKING:

STUFFING
CRANBERRY SAUCE
BREAD SAUCE

MAKE YOUR GRAVY BY TAKING 1 PINT OF FRESH STOCK AND ADDING 3 HEAPED TEASPOONS OF BISTO GRAVY POWDER DISSOLVED IN ONE CUP OF COLD WATER. BRING THE MIXTURE TO

THE BOIL WHISKING IT AND ADD A KNOB OF BUTTER TO LESSEN THE MIXTURE. TASTE AND ADD SALT AND PEPPER.

VEGETABLES:

BRUSSELS – COOK FOR 15 MINUTES IN SALTED BOILING WATER
FRENCH BEANS – COOK FOR 10 MINUTES IN SALTED BOILING WATER
BROCCOLI – COOK FOR 10 MINUTES IN SALTED BOILING WATER

YOU CAN MELT SOME BUTTER AND ADD SALT AND PEPPER AND TURN THE VEGETABLES IN THE PAN IN IT AND THEN SERVE.

I LIKE TO COOK ALL VEGETABLES WELL.

AIM TO EAT BETWEEN 3-4PM IN THE AFTERNOON.

VEGETARIAN CHRISTMAS

PEPPERS STUFFED WITH QUORN
BRUSSEL SPROUTS WITH CHESTNUTS
RED CABBAGE BRAISED WITH ORANGES AND CINNAMON
COURGETTE STICKS ROLLED IN SAGE AND ONION STUFFING
SMALL POTATO CUBES IN ROSEMARY AND HOT PAPRIKA CREAM

PEPPERS
CUT A RED PEPPER IN HALF AND LAY ON A BAKING SHEET
REMOVING THE SEEDS AND PUT IN OLIVE OIL AND A SQUARE OF
QUORN AND BLACK PEPPER AND ROAST FOR 45 MINUTES AT 220
CENTIGRADE UNTIL PEPPERS ARE BLACK AND CRISPY AT THE EDGES.

BRUSSEL SPROUTS
COOK BRUSSELS FOR ABOUT 15 MINUTES THEN FRY IN BUTTER IN A
SAUCEPAN WITH A DRAINED CAN OF CHESTNUTS AND ADD SALT
AND PEPPER TO TASTE.

RED CABBAGE
FINELY CHOP RED CABBAGE AND AN ONION AND FRY WITH
CINNAMON. ADD SALT AND PEPPER AND ½ PINT OF FRESH ORANGE
JUICE. COOK IN A CASSEROLE DISH FOR 1 ½ HOURS AT 200
CENTIGRADE.

COURGETTE

CHOP COURGETTES INTO STICKS AND DIP IN BEATEN EGG. ROLL IN DRY PAXO SAGE AND ONION STUFFING MIX WHICH HASN'T BEEN REHYDRATED AND FRY UNTIL GOLDEN IN BUTTER AND SUNFLOWER OIL.

POTATOES

PEEL POTATOES AND CUBE. ADD TO 2 PINTS OF DOUBLE CREAM. ADD SALT. ADD 2 TEASPOONS OF HOT PAPRIKA AND 1 TEASPOON OF DRIED ROSEMARY. COOK IN A HOT OVEN FOR ABOUT 1 HOUR.

CHRISTMAS PUDDING

2 PINT PUDDING BASIN AND A FEW SMALL ONES

1 PACKET OF ATORA (SUET)

½ LB OF CURRANTS

1LB OF RAISINS

1LB OF SULTANAS

4 OUNCES OF FLAKED ALMONDS

6 OUNCES OF GROUND ALMONDS

5 EGGS

6 OUNCES OF SELF RAISING FLOUR

1 PACKET OF MELTED SALTED BUTTER

½ BOTTLE OF BRANDY

6 OUNCES OF SOFT BROWN SUGAR

MIX TOGETHER AND MAKE A WISH IF YOU FEEL LIKE A WISH.

PUT IN THE LARGE PUDDING BASIN UP TO ONE THIRD FROM THE TOP AND THEN FILL THE LITTLE BASINS THE SAME WAY UNTIL YOU HAVE NO MORE LEFT. TIE SOME GREASEPROOF PAPER OVER THE TOP OF THE BASINS AND THEN PRESS ROUND SOME TIN FOIL COVERING WHOLE OF THE TOP OF THE BASINS. PUT THEM INTO A SAUCEPAN AND FILL UP THE SAUCEPAN TO A THIRD OF THE HEIGHT OF THE PUDDING BASINS AND BRING TO THE BOIL AND BOIL FOR ONE AND A HALF HOURS. YOU HAVE TO KEEP A VERY CAREFULL EYE ON THE PAN TO MAKE SURE IT DOESN'T BOIL DRY.

BRANDY WHITE SAUCE

2 OUNCES BUTTER

1 OUNCE PLAIN FLOUR PREFERABLY BUT ANY FLOUR WILL DO

4 OUNCES WHITE SUGAR

15 FLUID OUNCES OF MILK

5 FLUID OUNCES OF SINGLE CREAM

A GOOD DASH OF BRANDY

MELT THE BUTTER AND ADD THE FLOUR AND COOK OVER HEAT WITH A WHISK FOR A FEW SECONDS, STIRRING CONSTANTLY. ADD MILK AND SUGAR AND BRANDY AND BRING TO THE BOIL AND SIMMER FOR A MINUTE. THEN ADD THE CREAM AND SERVE.

BRANDY BUTTER OR RUM BUTTER

16 OUNCES/2 PACKETS OF VERY SOFT BUT NOT MELTED BUTTER

KEEP BUTTER OUT ALL DAY IN THE KITCHEN. MIX WITH 10 OUNCES OF ICING SUGAR AND GRADUALLY ADD IN AT THE END THE ROOM TEMPERATURE BRANDY OR RUM.

LAST MINUTE CHRISTMAS CAKE

A DOUBLE LINING OF GREASEPROOF PAPER/BAKING PARCHMENT
ON YOUR CHOSEN CAKE TIN

1LB OF SULTANAS

1LB OF RAISINS

½ LB OF CHERRIES

½ LB OF FLAKED ALMONDS

½ LB OF GROUND ALMONDS

½ LB OF BROWN SUGAR

½ LB OF WHITE SUGAR

6 EGGS

6 OUNCES SELF RAISING FLOUR

1 SERVING SPOON OF VANILLA ESSENCE

½ LB OF CHOPPED HAZELNUTS

8 FLUID OUNCES OF SUNFLOWER OIL

½ BOTTLE OF RUM AND BRANDY

MIX ALL THE INGREDIENTS WELL TOGETHER IN A LARGE MIXING
BOWL

POUR INTO YOUR PREPARED CAKE TIN AND COVER WITH
MORE BAKING PARCHMENT AND BAKE FOR 2 ½ HOURS AT 180
CENTIGRADE.

PUT SOME WARMED APRICOT JAM ON TOP OF THE CAKE WHILE
IT IS STILL WARM AND THEN DECORATE IT WITH SOME NUTS AND
CHERRIES.

MINCE PIES

2 PACKETS OF READY ROLL SHORTCRUST PASTRY

2 FLUID OUNCES OF RUM

1 BOTTLE OF GOOD MINCEMEAT

1 EGG BEATEN FOR THE GLAZE ON THE PIES

2 OUNCES OF CASTER SUGAR

ROLL OUT THE PASTRY TO 3 MILLIMETERS THICKNESS AND ADD THE RUM TO THE MINCEMEAT. MAKE UP THE MINCE PIES BY NOT PUTTING TOO MUCH FILLING IN THE PIES. THAT WAY YOU CAN EAT MORE OF THEM.

SEAL THEM WITH PASTRY LIDS AND COVER THEM WITH EGG WASH AND COVER WITH A SPRINKLING OF SUGAR AND BAKE AT 220 CENTIGRADE FOR 20 MINUTES.

RUM TRIFLE

RUM ½ BOTTLE

2 PACKETS OF TRIFLE CAKES OR SPONGE FINGERS

1 PACKET OF STRAWBERRIES OR FROZEN RASPBERRIES

1 PACKET OF ORANGE JELLY WHICH YOU MAKE UP TO THE MANUFACTURER'S INSTRUCTIONS

CUSTARD

CREAM

FLAKED CHOCOLATE

PUT THE TRIFLE CAKES IN TO THE BOTTOM OF A PUDDING BASIN AND POUR OVER THE FRUIT AND THEN THE JELLY AND LEAVE TO SET IN A REFRIDGERATER.

MAKE THE CUSTARD AND LEAVE TO COOL.

POUR THE CUSTARD OVER THE JELLY AND THEN LEAVE UNTIL REALLY SET IN THE REFRIDGERATER.

WHISK THE CREAM UNTIL THICK PEAKS FORM BUT DO NOT OVERWHISK OR ELSE THE CREAM WILL TURN INTO BUTTER. THEN PUT THE CREAM ON TO THE CUSTARD.

DECORATE THE TRIFLE WITH STRAWBERRIES AND FLAKED CHOCOLATE.

TOFFEED ORANGES

1 SLAB OF TOFFEE – MELTED OVER LOW TO MEDIUM HEAT IN A SAUCEPAN WITH SOME BUTTER.

SEVERAL OF YOUR FAVOURITE ORANGES PEELED AND CUT THROUGH IN TO CIRCLES.

SYRUP – 1 PINT OF WATER AND 1 POUND OF SUGAR BOILED FOR BOILED FOR 10 MINUTES.

PUT ORANGES IN A DISH. POUR OVER TOFFEE AND THEN FORK THROUGH AND IMMEDIATELY POUR OVER HOT SYRUP.

CHOCOLATE FUDGE CAKE

1 SLAB OF TOFFEE

2 OUNCES OF BUTTER

½ PINT OF DOUBLE CREAM

4 EGGS

6 OUNCES SELF RAISING FLOUR

2 OUNCES OF GROUD ALMONDS

4 FLUID OUNCES OF VEGETABLE OIL

6 OUNCES OF DEMARARA SUGAR

MELT THE TOFFEE WITH SOME BUTTER OVER GENTLE HEAT. MIX ALL THE INGREDIENTS TOGETHER AND ADD TO THE BAKING TIN AND BAKE FOR 1 HOUR TO 1 ½ HOURS AT 180 CENTIGRADE.

SERVE WARM WITH BUTTER.

SULTANA AND VANILLA CHEESECAKE

A HANDFULL OF SULTANAS

½ BOTTLE OF CHEAP VANILLA ESSENCE

4 EGGS

4 OUNCES OF SUGAR

2 TUBS OF MARSCAPONE

1 TUB OF PHILADELPHIA CREAM CHEESE

6 OUNCES OF SELF RAISING FLOUR

LEMON FLAVOURING

1 PACKET OF SHORTCRUST PASTRY

LINE A DEEP FLAN DISH WITH THE PASTRY AND BAKE BLIND FOR 15 MINUTES AT 220 CENTIGRADE.

MIX TOGETHER ALL OF THE INGREDIENTS AND PUT INTO THE PASTRY CASE AND BAKE FOR 1 HOUR AT 150 CENTIGRADE OR UNTIL RAISED AND SET.

CHOCOLATE FUDGE CHEESECAKE

1 SLAB OF TOFFEE
1 PINT OF DOUBLE CREAM
¼ PACKET OF BUTTER
1 LARGE BAR OF DARK CHOCOLATE

MELT TOGETHER THE ABOVE INGREDIENTS ON A MEDIUM HEAT TAKING CARE NOT TO OVERHEAT AND THEREFORE CAUSING THE CHOCOLATE TO BURN AND SEPARATE.

WHEN COOL ADD TO 1 PACKET OF PHILADELPHIA CREAM CHEESE AND 4 EGGS AND 6 OUNCES OF SELF RAISING FLOUR.

POUR IN TO A DEEP BAKED BLIND PASTRY CASE AND BAKE IN THE OVEN AT 150 CENTIGRADE UNTIL SET AND RISEN.

CHOCOLATE FUDGE COOKIES

MAKE INTO ROUND SHAPES AND PRESS WITH A FORK

1 SLAB OF TOFFEE

200 GRAMMES CHOCOLATE

½ PACKET OF CHOCOLATE

½ PACKET OF BUTTER

2 TABLESPOONS GOLDEN SYRUP

¼ PINT OF CREAM

½ POUND OF PLAIN FLOUR

2 OUNCES OF ROLLED OATS

MELT TOFFEE AND CREAM AND CHOCOLATE AND BUTTER AND GOLDEN SYRUP TOGETHER IN A MICROWAVE ON FULL POWER FOR 1 MINUTE AND THEN A FURTHER MINUTE AND THEN 30 SECONDS AND STIR GENTLY TO INCORPORATE ALL THE INGREDIENTS AND ADD PLAIN FLOUR AND ROLLED OATS.

BAKE AT 200 CENTIGRADE FOR 10 MINUTES.

THE LOOSE ALL PLUMS
SECTION 2

FRIED STEAK WITH MUSHROOM SAUCE

½ THICK RUMP STEAK
FLOUR
SALT AND PEPPER
WILD PORCINI MUSHROOMS
CREAM
BEEF STOCK

PUT THE FLOUR ONTO A PLATE AND ADD A GENEROUS AMOUNT OF SALT AND PEPPER.

RUBB STEAK INTO THIS FLOUR.

FRY IN THE HOT OIL ON HIGH HEAT FOR 1 MINUTE THEN TURN HEAT DOWN TO A MEDIUM AND COOK FOR A FURTHER 5 MINUTES ON EACH SIDE.

PUT THE MUSHROOMS INTO BEEF STOCK AND BRING TO BOIL FOR FIVE MINUTES. ADD CREAM AND BOIL FOR 10 MINUTES. TASTE. ADD SALT AND PEPPER AND SERVE.

TURKEY FRICASSE

ALL THE LEFT OVER WHITE MEAT

ALL THE LEFT OVER DARK MEAT

GET YOUR FAVOURITE BBQ SAUCE AND MIX WITH THE DARK MEAT AND BAKE IN THE OVEN AT 220 CENTIGRADE FOR 25 MINUTES.

MAKE A WHITE SAUCE AND COOK THE WHITE MEAT IN IT FOR 10 MINUTES.

SERVE WITH MASHED POTATOES AND SWEETCORN.

TAGLIATELLE WITH WHITE FISH

1 POUND OF WHITE FISH
1 GLASS OF WHITE WINE
JUICE OF ½ A LEMON
½ PINT OF FISH STOCK
½ PINT OF CREAM
TAGLIATELLE

PUT ALL THE LIQUID INGREDIENTS INTO A SAUCEPAN AND ADD CAREFULLY CHECKED FOR FISH BONES FISH AND COOK AND SIMMER FOR 5 MINUTES. ADD SALT AND PEPPER TO TASTE.

COOK TAGLIATELLE AS PER MANUFACTURER'S INSTRUCTIONS AND MIX WITH THE WHITE SAUCE.

BOILED EGGS

PUT EGGS INTO COLD WATER. JUST ENOUGH WATER TO COVER.

BRING TO THE BOIL QUICKLY OVER HIGHEST HEAT.

BOIL FOR 4 ½ MINUTES FOR SOFT EGGS.

BOIL FOR 6 ½ MINUTES FOR SET EGGS.

SMOKED HADDOCK CURRY

2 ONIONS CHOPPED

1 TEASPOON OF TURMERIC

A PINCH OF CORIANDER

A PINCH OF CUMIN

1 TEASPOON FENUGEEK

A PINCH OF CAYENNE PEPPER

VEGETABLE OIL

1 PINT DOUBLE CREAM

1 POUND OF SMOKED HADDOCK OR COD

1 HANDFULL OF RAISINS

2 TEASPOONS OF BROWN SUGAR

SERVE WITH WHITE RICE

FRY THE CHOPPED ONIONS WITH SPICES. ADD THE BONED FISH AND BE CAREFULL TO CHECK FOR BONES. ADD RAISINS AND SUGAR AND COOK TOGETHER FOR A FEW MINUTES WITH THE CREAM ADDED.

COOK RICE ACCORDING TO THE MANUFACTURER'S INSTRUCTIONS.

SAUSAGE AND TOMATO CURRY

8 SAUSAGES – YOUR FAVOURITE VARIETY

2 CANS OF TOMATOES

1 PINCH OF GROUND CUMIN

1 PINCH OF GROUND CORIANDER

1 TEASPOON FENUGEEK

A PINCH OF CAYENNE PEPPER

A PINCH OF CINNAMON

1 TEASPOON TURMERIC

A FEW CARDAMOM PODS

VEGETABLE OIL

2 TEASPOONS OF SUGAR

A HANDFULL OF SULTANAS

2 ONIONS PEELED AND CHOPPED

COOK ONIONS AND SPICES WITH THE SAUSAGES. ADD THE SUGAR AND TOMATOES AND COOK FOR A FURTHER 15 MINUTES.

SERVE WITH RICE.

EGG CURRY

8 EGGS BOILED SOFT AND PEELED

ALMONDS 1 PACKET FLAKED

1 PINCH OF GROUND CORIANDER

1 PINCH OF GROUND CUMIN

1 TEASPOON OF GROUND FENUGEEK

1 PINCH OF CAYENNE PEPPER

1 PINCH OF CINNAMON

1 TEASPOON TURMERIC

1 PINT OF DOUBLE CREAM

1 HANDFULL OF RAISINS

1 TEASOON OF SUGAR

COOK HERBS AND ONION, SUGAR AND RAISINS FOR 5 MINUTES IN VEGETABLE OIL. ADD EGGS WHOLE AND HTEN ADD CREAM AND NUTS AND SIMMER FOR FIVE MINUTES.

SERVE WITH CHIPS.

CURRIED TOMATO AND AUBERGINE

A FEW CARDAMOM PODS

2 TEASPOONS SUGAR

1 TEASPOON OF TURMERIC

A PINCH OF CORIANDER

1 TEASPOON OF FENUGEEK

½ PINT VEGETABLE STOCK

½ PACKET OF BUTTER

1 AUBERGINE CHOPPED

6 PLUM TOMATOES

1 ONION CHOPPED

FRY THE ONION AND THE SPICES AND AUBERGINE AND PLUM TOMATOES ALL IN SOME VEGETABLE OIL. ADD THE SUGAR AND BUTTER AND VEGETABLE STOCK AND PUT IN THE OVEN AT 220 CENTIGRADE FOR 30 MINUTES OR IN A SLOW COOKER FOR 1 HOUR ON HIGH.

CURRIED POACHED SALMON

3 PINTS OF MILK

SEVERAL CARDAMOM PODS

1 BAYLEAF

A PINCH OF CUMIN

A PINCH OF CORIANDER

1 TEASPOON OF FENUGEEK

1 PINCH OF CAYENNE

2 WHOLE ONIONS

A FEW CLOVES

A FEW BLACK PEPPER CORNS

1 SALMON TO FIT A FISH KETTLE

OR

SALMON PIECES TO FIT INTO A SAUCEPAN

SAUTE THE SPICES IN THE FISH KETTLE OR SAUCEPAN WITH SUNFLOWER OIL. ADD FISH AND THEN MILK TO ONE THIRD THE WAY UP THE KETTLE OR THE SAUCEPAN. BRING TO SIMMERING POINT AND CONTINUE JUST TURNING OVER FOR 30 MINUTES FOR THE FISH KETTLE AND FOR THE SAUCEPAN. LEAVE IN THE LIQUID FOR 15 MINUTES.

MAYONNAISE

---

4 EGG YOLKS

THIRD OF A BOTTLE OF SUNFLOWER OIL/RAPESEED OIL

QUARTER OF A BOTTLE OF LIGHT OLIVE OIL

1 TEASPOON OF ENGLISH MUSTARD POWDER

2 SERVING SPOONS OF WHITE CIDER VINEGAR

SALT AND PEPPER

PUT THE EGG YOLKS IN TO A FOOD PROCESSER WITH THE VINEGAR AND MUSTARD POWDER AND PUT ON FULL POWER FOR 30 SECONDS. THEN WITH POWER STILL GOING DRIP IN THE LIGHT OLIVE OIL AND THE OTHER OIL. POUR THESE OILS IN VERY SLOWLY IN A SLOW TRICKLE AND YOUR FOOD PROCESSER SHOULD BEING TO PRODUCE A LOVELY LIGHT MAYONNAISE. SEASON THE MAYONNAISE WITH SALT AND PEPPER.

THIS CAN BE KEPT IN A REFRIDGERATOR FOR 2 DAYS BUT IS BEST EATEN ON THE DAY OF MAKING.

FISHCAKES

1 PACKET OF SHOP BOUGHT BREADCRUMBS

½ LB OF COD FILLET

½ LB OF SMOKED HADDOCK FILLET

1 TEASPOON OF ENGLISH MUSTARD POWDER

2 LARGE POTATOES, PEELED, BOILED AND MASHED WITH BUTTER SALT AND PEPPER

2 FLUID OUNCES OF DOUBLE CREAM

1 FLUID OUNCE OF WATER FROM THE POACHING PAN

2 EGGS BEATEN

PLAIN FLOUR

1 OUNCE OF BUTTER FOR FRYING

OIL FOR FRYING

FIRSTLY BOIL THE POTATOES. WHILE THEY ARE BOILING POACH THE TWO TYPES OF FISHES IN THE SAME WATER. (BRING A PAN OF WATER TO THE SIMMER AND ADD THE FISHES AND KEEP SIMMERING FOR 5 MINUTES). TAKE OUT THE FISH AND SET ASIDE IN A LARGE MIXING BOWL. CHECK FOR BONES. MASH THE POTATOES IN TO A FIRM MASH.

ADD THE MUSTARD POWDER TO THE DOUBLE CREAM AND ALSO ADD 1 FLUID OUNCE OF WATER FROM THE POACHING PAN AND MIX WELL. ADD THIS TO THE FISHES IN THE MIXING BOWL ALONG WITH THE MASH. MIX THE INGREDIENTS IN THE BOWL VERY WELL TOGETHER.

ADD SALT AND PEPPER AND GIVE IT ANOTHER MIX. FORM BALLS FROM THE FISH MIXTURE. BEAT EGGS WITH SOME SALT AND PEPPER AND ROLL THE FISH BALLS AROUND IN IT BEFORE COATING IT WITH THE BREADCRUMBS.

THEN FRY THE FISH BALLS IN THE OIL AND BUTTER MIXTURE UNTIL COOKED.

SPAGHETTI WITH HAM AND CHEESE

COOK YOUR SPAGHETTI FOR UP TO TWICE AS LONG AS IT SAYS ON THE PACKET. IT'S GENERALLY MUCH NICER FOR YOUR DIGESTIVE SYSTEM.

½ PINT OF DOUBLE CREAM

1 SMALL PACKET OF GRATED PARMESAN CHEESE

1 SMALL TEASPOON OF ENGLISH MUSTARD

3 SLICES OF GOOD HAM – SMOKED IF YOU PREFER IT

1 TUB OF CREME FRAICHE

A TIN OF PEAS

IN A SAUCEPAN HEAT THE DOUBLE CREAM, THE CREME FRAICHE, THE CHOPPED HAM, THE DRAINED PEAS AND THE ENGLISH MUSTARD UNTIL PIPING HOT AND ADD THE WELL DRAINED SPAGHETTI. WHEN THOROUGHLY INCORPORATED ADD THE PARMESAN CHEESE AND ROUGHLY MIX.

SERVE ALL ON IT'S OWN OR WITH CRUSTY BREAD AND BUTTER.

RICE WITH MUSHROOMS AND CREAM SAUCE

1 TABLESPOON MUSHROOM KETCHUP
PACKET OF RICE
10 FLUID OUNCES OF DOUBLE CREAM
½ PINT OF CHICKEN OR VEGETABLE STOCK
200 GRAMMES OF VALUE MUSHROOMS
A LITTLE BUTTER AND A DASH OF OIL
SALT AND PEPPER

BOIL THE RICE UNTIL TENDER WITH NO SALT ADDED. IN A SEPARATE SAUCEPAN ADD SOME BUTTER AND A LITTLE OIL AND SAUTE THE CHOPPED MUSHROOMS – YOU CAN WASH THEM IF YOU LIKE BUT A WIPE OF THEM WILL SO. WHEN THEY ARE BROWNING ADD THE STOCK AND THE DOUBLE CREAM AND BRING TO THE BOIL. REDUCE THE MIXTURE BY BOILING FOR ABOUT 4 – 5 MINUTES THEN ADD THE MUSHROOM KETCHUP AND ADD TO THE RICE.

SERVE WITH A ROAST CHICKEN OR SIMPLY ON IT'S OWN. PERSONALLY I WOULD CHEAT AND BY A BBQ CHICKEN.

SCRAMBLED EGGS

ROUGHLY SPEAKING YOU NEED 2-3 LARGE EGGS PER PERSON

A LITTLE SALT AND QUITE A LOT OF BLACK PEPPER

SOME BUTTER IN A SAUCEPAN

TAKE THE BUTTER IN THE SAUCEPAN AND ADD THE SALT AND PEPPER. HEAT UNTIL THE BUTTER IS FOAMING AND THEN CRACK IN THE EGGS. MIX WITH A WOODEN SPOON QUITE QUICKLY OVER A BRISK HEAT, UNTIL SOFT. TAKE OFF HEAT AND KEEP STIRRING. SERVE WITH TOAST.

POTATO SOUP

4 LARGE POTATOES

1 POT OF SOUR CREAM

1 PINT OF VEGETABLE STOCK

3 LARGE ONIONS

SALT AND PEPPER

BUTTER AND OIL FOR FRYING

THIS IS A THICK SOUP WHICH LITERALLY HOLDS ON TO THE SPOON ITSELF. POTATOES ARE A VERY GOOD SOURCE OF VITAMINS WHICH IS WHY CHIPS (POMMES FRITES) ARE SO GOOD FOR YOU.

PEEL THE POTATOES AND ROUGHLY CHOP THEM AND PEEL AND ROUGHLY CHOP THE ONIONS. ADD THEM ALL TO A SAUCEPAN WITH SOME BUTTER AND OIL AND SAUTE THEM FOR A GOOD 10 MINUTES STIRRINGWELL. IF THE POTATO STARTS TO STICK JUST ADD THE VEGETABLE STOCK STRAIGHT AWAY. COOK WELL AND WHEN THE POTATOES ARE READY PUT IT ALL INTO A FOOD PROCESSER AND TURN UP THE VOLUME. ADD THE SOUR CREAM AFTER THE POTATOES HAVE BEEN WHIRLED AND RETURNED TO THE SAUCEPAN. ADD ENOUGH STOCK TO MAKE THE SOUP TO YOUR REQUIRED CONSISTENCY AND FINALLY THEN ADD SALT AND PEPPER.

CARROT AND GINGER SOUP

2 POUNDS OF CARROTS PEELED AND CHOPPED

1 TEASPOON OF FRESH GRATED GINGER

A HANDFULL OF RAISINS

A PINCH OF CORIANDER

1 LARGE ONION PEELED AND ROUGHLY CHOPPED

1 PINT OF VEGETABLE STOCK

1 TEASPOON OF BROWN SUGAR

1 MEDIUM POTATO

A LITTLE OIL AND BUTTER TO COOK WITH

PUT THE CARROTS AND ONIONS AND POTATOES IN A SAUCEPAN WITH SOME OIL AND BUTTER AND FRY. AFTER A FEW MINTES ADD THE GRATED GINGER AND RAISINS, BROWN SUGAR AND VEGETABLE STOCK.

COOK DOWN FOR A WHILE ADDING THE STOCK AND WATER AS NECESSARY AND WHEN THE CARROTS ARE COOKED PUREE THE WHOLE LOT IN A FOOD PROCESSER.

ADD SALT AND PEPPER TO SUIT YOUR TASTES. YOU CAN ADD A LITTLE MILK BEFORE YOU FINISH COOKING TO ADD A LITTLE CREAMY CONSISTENCY.

CHICKEN LIVER PATE

8 OUNCES OF CHICKEN LIVERS

2 MANDARINS

1 ONION

2 SERVINGSPOONS OF BRANDY

1 SERVINGSPOON OF SOFT BROWN SUGAR

2 PACKETS OF BUTTER

2 CLOVES OF GARLIC – DON'T COOK IT

SALT AND PEPPER

IN A SAUCEPAN PUT SOME OIL AND BUTTER AND FRY THE ONION AND CHICKEN LIVERS. ADD SOME BRANDY AND BROWN SUGAR AND SALT AND PEPPER AND COOK AGAIN FOR A FEW MINUTES. TAKE OFF THE HEAT AND ADD THE MANDARIN AND GARLIC AND MORE BUTTER. PUT IN THE FOOD PROCESSOR WITH SOME MORE BUTTER.

THEN PUT IN TO A BOWL AND COVER WITH MELTED BUTTER AND LEAVE TO SET.

MONKFISH CURRY

2 TAILS OF MONKFISH

A HANDFULL OF SULTANAS

1 PINT OF CREAM

1 TEASPOON OF TURMERIC

1 TEASPOON OF FENUGEEK

2 STAR ANAISE

A PINCH OF CUMIN

1 CHOPPED ONION

1 CHOPPED BANANA

1 CAN OF LYCHEES – DRAINED

FRY THE TURMERIC, FENUGEEK, STAR ANAISE, CUMIN, ONION, BANANA AND LYCHEES IN SOME VEGETABLE OIL AND THEN ADD THE CREAM AND COOK DOWN FOR 2 MINUTES AND THEN ADD THE MONKFISH TAILS AND COOK THROUGH FOR 5 MINUTES.

SERVE WITH CHIPS.

.

THE LOOSE ALL PLUMS
SECTION 3

WALNUT AND HAZELNUT GALETTE

1 OUNCE OF CASTER SUGAR

2 OUNCES OF WALNUTS GROUND

2 OUNCES OF HAZELNUTS GROUND

1 OUNCE OF PLAIN FLOUR

3 OUNCES OF COLD BUTTER

1 PINT OF DOUBLE CREAM WHIPPED WITH 1 FLUID OUNCE OF GRAND MARNIER AND 1 OUNCE OF ICING SUGAR

1 LB OF RASPBERRIES

IN A FOOD PROCESSER MIX THE CASTER SUGAR, WALNUTS, HAZELNUTS, PLAIN FLOUR AND BUTTER UNTIL A PASTRY IS FORMED.

DIVIDE THE PASTRY IN TO THREE AND ROLL THEM OUT IN TO THE SAME SIZED ROUNDS WHICH ARE VERY THIN.

PUT EACH OF THEM ON TO A BAKING SHEET AND BAKE AT 220 CENTIGRADE FOR 8 MINUTES. WHEN COOL FILL THEM AND MAKE A TOWER WITH THEM.

STRAWBERRY MERINGUE

1 DRY MERINGUE BASE
2 PACKETS OF STRAWBERRIES
1 PACKET OF GINGER BISCUITS
1 PINT OF DOUBLE CREAM
2 OUNCES OF ICING SUGAR
MINT LEAVES

BREAK UP THE GINGER BISCUITS AND MERINGUE INTO LARGE CHUNKS AND PUT THEM IN A BASIN AND POUR OVER HALF OF THE DOULBE CREAM AND LEAVE TO SOAK IN. CUP UP 1 PACKET OF STRAWBERRIES ROUGHLY. ADD TO THE GINGER BISCUITS AND MERINGUE AND LEAVE TO SOAK AGAIN. PUREE THE OTHER STRAWBERRIES AND WHIP THE OTHER PINT OF DOUBLE CREAM WITH THE ICING SUGAR AND MIX WITH THE GINGER AND STRAWBERRY MIXTURE.

FOLD ALL THE CREAM IN GENTLY OTHERWISE YOU WILL MAKE BUTTER SO DO NOT OVERFOLD.

PUT INTO GLASS DISHES AND CHILL OVERNIGHT. DECORATE WITH MINT LEAVES.

PEACHES AND CUSTARD CREAM

1 PACK OF PEACHES

10 FLUID OUNCES OF SOUR CREAM

10 FLUID OUNCES OF DOUBLE CREAM

1 PINT OF CUSTARD

1 PACKET OF AMARETTI BISCUITS (ITALIAN BISCUITS)

HALF A JAR OF BONNE MAMAN PEACH COMPOTE

LAYER THE AMARETTI BISCUITS IN A PUDDING BASIN. CUT UP THE PEACHES INTO SLICES AND PLACE ON TOP OF THE BISCUITS. POUR OVER THE DOUBLE CREAM. PUT THE SOUR CREAM, CUSTARD AND PEACH COMPOTE IN A BOWL TOGETHER AND MIX. PUT OVER THE TOP OF THE PEACH SLICES AND BISCUITS. CHILL OVERNIGHT.

BLACK CHERRY AND CHOCOLATE SPONGE

6 OUNCES OF SELF RAISING FLOUR

6 OUNCES OF BROWN SUGAR

4 OUNCES BLACK CHERRIES

200 GRAM BAR OF DARK CHOCOLATE

6 OUNCES OF BUTTER MELTED

3 EGGS

BREAK UP THE CHOCOLATE AND MELT IN THE MICROWAVE ON FULL POWER FOR ONE MINUTE. STONE THE CHERRIES OR JUST DRAIN A CAN OF CHERRIES AND PUT ALL OF THE INGREDIENTS IN TO A BOWL AND MIX.

WHEN MIXED TOGETHER PUT INTO A PUDDING BASIN AND PLACE A PIECE OF GREASEPROOF PAPER OVER THE TOP AND TIE IT DOWN AROUND THE PUDDING BASIN LIP. THEN PUT TIN FOIL OVER THE TOP AND SCRUNCH IT ROUND THE SIDES OF THE PUDDING BASIN LIP.

PLACE THE PUDDING BASIN INTO A PAN OF WATER WHICH COMES A THIRD OF THE WAY UP THE SIDE OF THE PUDDING BASIN AND THEN COMMENCE TO BOIL THE WATER ALWAYS KEEPING AN EYE ON THE WATER LEVEL OF THE SAUCEPAN BECAUSE IF IT BOILS DRY YOU HAVE GOT A BURN'T PUDDING AND SAUCEPAN.

IT IS A DELICIOUS PUDDING SERVED WITH CREAM AND CUSTARD – PREFERABLY MIXED TOGETHER.

MELTED TOFFEE AND A
WHIRL OF STRAWBERRY

2 TABLESPOONS OF GOLDEN SYRUP

1 PACK OF STRAWBERRIES

1 PINT OF WHIPPING CREAM - WHIPPED

1 PINT OF CUSTARD

1 SLAB OF TOFFEE

4 OUNCES OF BUTTER

MELT THE BUTTER AND THE TOFFEE TOGETHER OVER A GENTLE HEAT
AND WHEN MELTED ADD THE GOLDEN SYRUP. WHILE STILL WARM BUT
NOT HOT ADD THE CUSTARD AND MIX WELL. WHEN COLD FOLD IN
THE WHIPPED CREAM AND THE ROUGHLY CHOPPED STRAWBERRIES.

DEORATE WITH SOME CHOCOLATE.

BLACKCURRANT AND BANANA ROSE DESSERT

1 JAR OF BLACKCURRANT COMPOTE

3 FLUID OUNCES OF ORANGE JUICE

1 PINT OF CUSTARD

1 PACKET OF SPONGE FINGERS

1 PINT OF DOUBLE CREAM

4 LARGE RIPE BANANAS

3 OUNCES OF SOFT BROWN SUGAR

4 OUNCES OF BUTTER

MINT LEAVES

FRY THE BANANAS IN THE BUTTER AND THE SUGAR UNTIL THEY HAVE COOKED WELL BUT STILL RETAIN SOME SHAPE THEN ADD 2 SERVING SPOONS OF THE BLACKCURRANT COMPOTE AND STIR THROUGH WHILE THE BANANAS ARE STILL HOT. WHIP THE DOUBLE CREAM UNTIL SOFT PEAKS FORM AND ADD TO THE CUSTARD. WHEN THE BANANA MIXTURE IS COLD ADD THE CREAM AND CUSTARD MIXTURE AND FOLD IN. BREAK UP THE FINGERS AND MIX THEM WITH THE REST OF THE BLACKCURRANT COMPOTE AND THE ORANGE JUICE AND PUT THEM IN THE BOTTOM OF THE SERVING DISH AND THEN PUT THE BANANA MIXTURE ON TOP. CHILL OVERNIGHT AND DECORATE WITH MINT LEAVES.

DATE AND GINGER CAKE

4 OUNCES OF GROUND ALMONDS

1 TEASPOON OF GROUND GINGER

100 GRAMMES OF SOFTENED DATES

4 OUNCES OF SELF RAISING FLOUR

4 FLUID OUNCES OF VEGETABLE OIL

A PINCH OF ALLSPICE

2 OUNCES OF DEMARARA SUGAR

3 EGGS

2 OUNCES OF SOFT BUTTER

CHOP THE DATES UNTIL VERY SMALL IN A FOOD PROCESSER. PUT ALL THE INGREDIENTS IN A LARGE MIXING BOWL AND MIX. ADD SOME WARM MILK IF THE MIXTURE NEEDS TO BE SOFTENED A LITTLE. PUT INTO A LOOSE BOTTOMED CAKE TIN AND BAKE AT 180 CENTIGRADE FOR ABOUT AN HOUR OR UNTIL A KNIFE COMES OUT CLEAN.

IT IS GOOD WITH A BIT OF BUTTER.

CARROT AND PINEAPPLE CAKE

4 LARGE PEELED AND GRATED CARROTS

1 SMALL CAN OF CHOPPED PINEAPPLE

6 FLUID OUNCES OF VEGETABLE OIL

3 EGGS

6 OUNCES OF SOFT DARK SUGAR

4 OUNCES OF SELF RAISING FLOUR

SALT

1 TUB OF PHILADELPHIA SOFT CHEESE

4 OUNCES OF ICING SUGAR

4 OUNCES OF SOFT REAL BUTTER

PUT ALL THE CAKE INGREDIENTS INTO A LARGE MIXING BOWL AND MIX THOROUGHLY. PUT IN A DEEP LOOSE BOTTOMED CAKE TIN AND BAKE IN THE OVEN AT 180 CENTIGRADE FOR 1 HOUR OR UNTIL A KNIFE COMES OUT CLEANLY.

TO MAKE THE ICING MIX THE BUTTER AND ICING SUGAR AND THEN ADD THE CREAM CHEESE AND GENTLY FOLD IT IN.

WHEN THE CAKE IS VERY COLD PUT THE ICING ON THE TOP.

WALNUT AND HAZELNUT ORANGE CAKE

100 GRAMMES OF WALNUTS CHOPPED

100 GRAMMES OF HAZELNUTS CHOPPED

A JAR OF STRONG OXFORD MARMALADE

3 EGGS

4 OUNCES OF SELF RAISING FLOUR

4 OUNCES OF SOFT BUTTER

4 OUNCES OF SOFT BROWN SUGAR

3 FLUID OUNCES OF VEGETABLE OIL

MIX ALL THE INGREDIENTS TOGETHER IN A LARGE MIXING BOWL. POUR INTO A LOOSE BOTTOMED CAKE TIN AND BAKE AT 180 CENTIGRADE FOR ABOUT 1 HOUR OR UNTIL A KNIFE COMES OUT CLEAN.

ENJOY WARM WITH BUTTER.

DROP SCONES

1 EGG

2 ½ OUNCES OF PLAIN FLOUR

1 OUNCE OF SUGAR

A HANDFULL OF SUTANAS

5 FLUID OUNCES OF SOUR CREAM

1 TEASPOON OF BAKING POWDER

A LITTLE MILK

MIX ALL THE INGREDIENTS TOGETHER AND BEAT WITH A WHISK. THE RESULTING MIXTURE SHOULD BE A CREAMY TEXTURE AND HOLD THE BACK OF A SPOON WELL.

HEAT A LITTLE BUTTER AND VEGETABLE OIL IN A FRYING PAN AND WHEN IT IS SIZZLING ADD TEASPOONS FULL OF THE MIXTURE TO THE PAN. COOK UNTIL BROWN ON BOTH SIDES AND ENJOY WHILE STILL WARM WITH BUTTER AND STRAWBERRY JAM.

ALMOND COFFEE CAKE

200 GRAMMES OF GROUND ALMONDS

6 OUNCES OF WARMED BUTTER

7 OUNCES OF GRANULATED SUGAR

2 OUNCES OF GRANULATED SUGAR SEPARATELY FOR THE MERINGUE

4 EGGS

VANILLA ESSENCE

5 OUNCES OF SELF RAISING FLOUR

6 TEASPOONS OF COFFEE DISSOLVED IN A CUP OF BOILING WATER

FOR THE ICING YOU WILL NEED TO TAKE ONE PACKET OF SOFT REAL BUTTER AND BEAT IT WITH 6 OUNCES OF ICING SUGAR AND THEN SOME VANILLA ESSENCE AND THEN CAREFULLY FOLD IN 1 PACKET OF PHILADELPHIA SOFT CREAM CHEESE.

FOR THE CAKE:

SEPARATE THE EGGS. MIX ALL THE DRY INGREDIENTS TOGETHER EXCEPT FOR THE 2 OUNCES OF GRANULATED SUGAR AND ADD THE COOLED COFFEE AND THE BUTTER AND THE EGG YOLKS AND MIX WELL. WHIP THE EGG WHITES AND THEN ADD THE REMAINING SUGAR AND BEAT WELL AGAIN AND THEN ADD THE VANILLA ESSENCE AND BEAT AGAIN AND FOLD IN TO THE CAKE MIXTURE. BAKE FOR AN HOUR AT THE TEMPERATURE OF 180 CENTIGRADE OR UNTIL A KNIFE COMES OUT CLEANLY.

LET THE CAKE COOL AND ICE IT AND DECORATE WITH SOME SUGARED FRUITS.

CHOCOLATE ROULADE

2 PINTS OF DOUBLE CREAM WHIPPED WITH 1 OUNCE OF ICING SUGAR

1 TIN OF CHERRY COMPOTE OR PIE FILLING

3 EGGS

1 OUNCE OF COCOA POWDER

6 OUNCES OF SOFT BROWN SUGAR

6 OUNCES OF SELF RAISING FLOUR

A POT OF GREEK YOGUART

6 OUNCES OF REAL BUTTER

1 LARGE BAR OF DARK CHOCOLATE

SEPARATE THE EGGS. MELT THE CHOCOLATE BY PUTTING IT IN TO A MICROWAVE ON FULL POWER FOR 1 MINUTE. PUT THE EGG YOLKS, YOGUART, BUTTER, CHOCOLATE AND DRY INGREDIENTS IN TO A MIXING BOWL AND MIX TOGETHER WELL. WHISK THE EGG WHITES AND FOLD THEM INTO THE CAKE MIXTURE AND POUR IT INTO A SWISS ROLL TIN WHICH HAS BEEN LINED WITH BAKING PARCHMENT AND BAKE AT 180 CENTIGRADE FOR 30 MINUTES.

AFTER THE CAKE HAS COOLED SPREAD THE TOP LIGHTLY WITH THE CHERRY COMPOTE OR PIE FILLING AND THEN WITH A LITTLE BIT OF THE CREAM AND ROLL FROM ONE SIDE TO THE OTHER LIFTING THE BAKING PARCHMENT OFF AS YOU ROLL IT ROUND AND ROLL IT ON TO A PLATE.

FOR THE REST OF THE CREAM WITH THE 1 OUNCE OF ICING SUGAR PILE IT ON TOP OF THE SWISS ROLL AND DECORATE WITH COCOA POWDER.

FREEZER ICECREAM

2 PINTS OF DOUBLE CREAM

3 EGGS

14 OUNCES OF GRANULATED SUGAR

8 OUNCES OF FROZEN RASPBERRIES OR ANY FRUIT

VANILLA ESSENCE

USE 8 OUNCES OF THE GRANULATED SUGAR AND HEAT WITH THE FRUIT UNTIL THE SUGAR IS MELTED AND THEN PASS IT THROUGH A SIEVE. WHIP THE DOUBLE CREAM. WHIP THE EGG YOLK WITH 3 OUNCES OF GRANULATED SUGAR UNTIL A THICK STRAND APPEARS IN THE LIQUID. WHIP THE EGG WHITES UNTIL PEAKS FORM AND THEN ADD 3 OUNCES OF GRANULATED SUGAR AND WHIP INTO A MERINGUE. FOLD EVERYTHING TOGETHER AND FREEZE FOR 3 HOURS.

A RULER'S BIRTHDAY CAKE

STRONG FRESH COFFEE

4 EGGS

4 OUNCES OF SELF RAISING FLOUR

4 OUNCES OF GROUND ALMONDS

4 FLUID OUNCES OF WHISKY

4 FLUID OUNCES OF RUM

8 OUNCES OF SOFT DARK BROWN SUGAR

VANILLA

½ BOTTLE OF MAPLE SYRUP

6 OUNCES OF BUTTER

2 FLUID OUNCES OF VEGETABLE OIL

PUT EVERYTHING INTO A LARGE MIXING BOWL AND MIX WELL TOGETHER.

POUR INTO A LARGE BAKINGTIN AND COOK AT 180 CENTIGRADE FOR 1 HOUR OR UNTIL A KNIFE COMES OUT CLEAN.

COVER WITH CREAM WHIPPED WITH ICING SUGAR AND BRANDY WHEN OUT OF THE OVEN AND COLD.

THE LOOSE ALL PLUMS
SECTION 4

SHEPHERDS PIE

BOIL SOME POTATOES WITHOUT SALT AND MAKE A MASH USING SOME BUTTER, A LITTLE MILK AND SOME SALT AND PEPPER.

MEANWHILE FRY A ROUGHLY CHOPPED ONION AND A ROUGHLY CHOPPED CARROT IN SOME VEGETABLE OIL. WHEN THEY ARE SOFT AND SLIGHTLY COLOURED ADD THE MINCE AND FRY UNTIL THE COLOUR HAS CHANGED. SPRINKLE OVER 2 CUBES OF OXO AND A HEAPED DESSERT SPOON OF BISTO WHICH HAS BEEN DISSOLVED IN A CUP OF WATER AND SIMMER UNTIL IT HAS REDUCED INTO A THICK MEAT SAUCE. ADD SALT AND PEPPER.

POUR THE MEAT SAUCE INTO A CASSEROLE DISH AND ADD THE MASH ON TOP, ALL OVER IT, SCORING IT ON TOP OF IT WITH A FORK. PUT SOME CHEDDAR ON TOP OF THAT AND BAKE IN THE OVEN AT 220 CENTIGRADE FOR 40 MINUTES OR UNTIL THE CHEESE ON TOP HAS GONE GOLDEN BROWN.

SERVE WITH SOME PEAS – IF YOU DO WANT ANY VEGETABLES WITH IT.

SPAGHETTI WITH MEAT SAUCE

FRY ROUGHLY CHOPPED ONIONS IN 2 TABLESPOONS OF VEGETABLE OIL AND THEN ADD MINCE AND BROWN. CRUMBLE IN AN OXO CUBE AND ADD A CAN OF PLUM TOMATOES AND A HEAPED DESSERT SPOON OF GRAVY POWDER DISSOLVED IN HALF A CUP OF WATER AND COOK UNTIL A THICK SAUCE HAS FORMED. DON'T FORGET TO ADD SOME SEASONINGS.

COOK THE SPAGHETTI ACCORDING TO YOUR TASTE WITH SALT. IT SHOULD TAKE 10 MINUTES LONGER THAN IT SAYS ON THE PACKET.

SERVE WITH YOUR FAVOURITE CHEESE TO BE SPINKLED ON THE TOP.

CAULIFLOWER CHEESE

MAKE A CHEESE SAUCE WITH 13 FLUID OUNCES OF MILK.

FIRST MELT 1 OUNCE OF BUTTER AND THEN ADD A HEAPED TABLESPOON OF FLOUR AND MIX IN TO THE BUTTER AND THEN ADD THE 13 FLUID OUNCES OF MILK. USE A WHISK TO MAKE SURE THAT LUMPS DON'T FORM AS IT IS COOKING. LET IT SIMMER FOR ABOUT 1 MINUTE AND ADD SOME GRATED CHEDDAR AND THEN SEASON TO YOUR TASTE. USE A PACKET SAUCE IF YOU LIKE IT BETTER.

CUT UP THE CAULIFLOWER AND DON'T BE TOO CAREFULL ABOUT HOW – JUST LEAVE OUT THE STALK AND COOK THE CAULIFLOWER IN SALTED BOILING WATER FOR ABOUT 10 MINUTES UNTIL A KNIFE GOES INTO IT EASILY.

DRAIN THE CAULIFLOWER AND POUR OVER THE CHEESE SAUCE AND MIX TOGETHER QUITE ROUGHLY.

PUT ON A PLATE WITH HAM AND MUSTARD.

YOU CAN ALSO DO THIS WITH BROCCOLI.

MACARONI CHEESE

1 BOILED EGG PER PERSON
CHEESE SAUCE FROM RECIPE FOR CAULIFLOWER CHEESE
MACARONI

MAKE UP THE CHEESE SAUCE AND COOK THE MACARONI UNTIL QUITE SOFT. POUR THE CHEESE SAUCE ALL OVER THE MACARONI AND ADD THE HALVED EGGS IN A SERVING DISH. PUT A LAYER OF GRATED CHEESE ON TOP AND BAKE IN THE OVEN AT 220 CENTIGRADE UNTIL THE TOP IS GOLDEN BROWN.

SERVE WITH SOME CRUSTY BREAD.

STEAK AND KIDNEY PIE

HALF A POUND OF CHOPPED STEWING STEAK PER PERSON
4 LAMBS KIDNEYS
ONIONS
GRAVY POWDER
2 PACKETS OF FLAKY PASTRY

FRY THE KIDNEYS IN OIL AT QUITE A HIGH TEMPERATURE BRISKLY UNTIL COOKED LIGHTLY THROUGH AND BROWNED.

FRY ONIONS AND THEN STEWING STEAK WHICH HAS BEEN COATED WITH SEASONED FLOUR IN THE SAME FRYING PAN. PUT THE KIDNEYS, ONIONS AND STEWING STEAK IN THE SLOW COOKER AND SET ON HIGH FOR THREE AND A HALF HOURS.

AFTER COOKING THE MEAT IN THE SLOW COOKER PUT IT INTO A PIE DISH AND COVER WITH ROLLED OUT THIN FLAKY PASTRY AND CUT A CROSS IN THE MIDDLE. YOU CAN DECORATE THE TOP WITH SOME OF THE LEFT OVER PASTRY. GLAZE WITH A BEATEN EGG AND SPRINKLE OVER SOME FINE SALT CRYSTALS AND BAKE FOR 35 – 45 MINUTES AT 200 CENTIGRADE OR UNTIL GOLDEN BROWN.

SERVE WITH MASHED POTATOES AND PEAS.

CHICKEN AND MUSHROOM PIE

2 PACKETS OF FLAKY PASTRY

1 CHICKEN BREAST PER PERSON

3 MUSHROOMS PER PERSON

LIGHT SOY SAUCE

1 LARGE ONION

GRAVY POWDER

PARSLEY

SALT AND PEPPER

FRY THE ONIONS AND ADD THE CHICKEN WHICH HAS BEEN CHOPPED INTO LARGE PIECES AND THEN ADD THE CLEANED ROUGHLY CHOPPED MUSHROOMS.

ADD A GENEROUS AMOUNT OF SOY SAUCE AND ADD THE GRAVY POWDER – ONE DESSERT SPOON OF WHICH HAS BEEN DISSOLVED IN A CUP OF WATER TO THE COOKING PAN.

LET IT SIMMER FOR 1 MINUTE SO EVERYTHING IS COOKED THROUGH AND THEN ADD SOME PARSLEY AND SOME SALT AND PEPPER.

PUT INTO A PIE DISH AND ROLL OUT THE FLAKY PASTRY QUITE THINLY AND PUT OVER THE TOP OF THE PIE DISH. YOU CAN DECORATE IT AS YOU LIKE THEN EGG GLAZE THE TOP WITH BEATEN EGG AND A SPRINKLING OF SALT.

BAKE IN THE OVEN FOR 45 MINUTES AT 200 CENTIGRADE UNTIL THE PASTRY IS GOLDEN BROWN.

FISH PIE

SMOKED HADDOCK

COD

PLEASE CHECK THE FISH THOROUGHLY FOR BONES

TOMATOES – SKINNED

MASHED POTATOES

BOILED EGGS

CHEESE SAUCE

PUT THE SMOKED HADDOCK AND COD INTO SIMMERING MILK AND KEEP MILK SIMMERING FOR 5 MINUTES. THEN DRAIN TAKING CARE TO KEEP THE MILK TO ONE SIDE. THEN USE THE MILK TO MAKE THE CHEESE SAUCE.

PUT THE TOMATOES IN TO BOILING WATER TO TAKE OFF THEIR SKINS.

CUT THE BOILED EGGS AND TOMATOES INTO QUARTERS.

PUT THE FISH INTO THE CHEESE SAUCE AND ADD THE EGGS AND TOMATOES AND MIX.

PUT INTO THE SERVING DISH AND COVER WITH MASHED POTATOES.

DOT THE PIE WITH BUTTER AND PUT IT IN TO THE OVEN AT 220 CENTIGRADE FOR 30 – 35 MINUTES OR UNTIL GOLDEN BROWN.

SALMON WITH PASTA

1 TUB OF MARSCAPONE

1 POUND OF FRESH SALMON

1 PACKET OF FRESH SPINACH

½ PINT OF DOUBLE CREAM

¼ PINT OF FISH STOCK

QUITE A LOT OF PARMESAN

VERMICELLI – COOK ACCORDING TO MANUFACTURER'S INSTRUCTIONS

A PINCH OF NUTMEG

BASIL LEAVES

POACH THE SALMON IN THE CREAM AND FISH STOCK AND ADD A PINCH OF NUTMEG AND THEN ADD THE SPINACH AND MARSCAPONE. BREAK UP THE BASIL LEAVES AND ADD TO THE DISH. SERVE THE VERMICELLI WITH THE SAUCE ON THE TOP AND SPRINKLED WITH PARMESAN.

MACARONI WITH WHITE WINE AND HERB SAUCE

MACARONI

WHITE WINE

SHALLOTS

ROSEMARY

FISH STOCK

CREAM

MAKE THE SAUCE BY REDUCING THE WHITE WINE WITH THE FISH STOCK AND THE CREAM AND THE ROSEMARY AND SEASON WITH SALT AND PEPPER.

SAUTE THE SHALLOTS SEPARATELY.

COOK THE MACARONI TO THE MANUFACTURER'S INSTRUCTIONS.

MIX THE MACARONI WITH THE SHALLOTS AND SERVE WITH THE CREAM SAUCE ON THE SIDE.

TUNA AND PIMENTO AND BEAN SALAD

TUNA
1 JAR PIMENTO (PEPPERS IN OIL)
BLACK EYED BEANS SOAKED OVERNIGHT IN WATER
OLIVE OIL
FISH STOCK
WHITE ONIONS FINELY CHOPPED

COOK THE BEANS IN THE SLOW COOKER WITH OLIVE OIL AND FISH STOCK FOR TWO AND A HALF HOURS ON HIGH. LEAVE UNTIL TEPID. ADD COOKED TUNA AND FINELY CHOPPED PIMENTO. ADD SOME PARSLEY AND CORIANDER AND SERVE SEVERAL HOURS LATER.

PHEASANT STEW

4 PHEASANTS SIMMERED FOR ¾ OF AN HOUR

1 DICED ONION

1 DICED CARROT

A HANDFULL OF REDCURRANTS

MACE

DOUBLE CREAM

PUT 1 PINT OF DOUBLE CREAM INTO A FRYING PAN WITH ¼ OF A PINT OF THE PHEASANT STOCK AND ADD THE ONIONS AND CARROTS AND REDCURRANTS AND MACE AND REDUCE FOR 5 MINUTES. TAKE THE BREASTS OFF THE PHEASANTS AND PLACE INTO THE PAN OF CREAM SAUCE AND WARM THROUGH. SEASON WITH SUGAR TO TASTE.

SERVE WITH CHIPS, FRIES OR MASHED POTATOES.

PHEASANT AND BANANA CREAM

4 PHEASANTS SIMMERED FOR ¾ OF AN HOUR

1 ONION FINELY CHOPPED

1 TEASPOON OF TURMERIC

FRESHLY CHOPPED CORIANDER

2 BANANAS

CREAM

TAKE THE MEAT OFF THE PHEASANTS AND ADD TO THE ONION FRIED IN THE PAN WITH THE TURMERIC, CHOPPED BANANAS AND CORIANDER. ADD THE CREAM AND SEASONING AND WARM THROUGH AND SERVE WITH RED RICE.

Lightning Source UK Ltd.
Milton Keynes UK
UKOW02f1910160516

274358UK00002B/164/P